Pearls In The Sun

By Belad Al-karkhey

To Ian,

I dedicate these words, these fragments of
my soul, to you.

We are ever seeking a life of passion, and
art, and music, and learning, and just
simply existing without fear of being
controlled by others. To have power over
our selves and how we choose to live the
one life we are able in these bodies.

You embodied the pursuit of seeking
individuality and control of your identity
through the movement of your art and
creativity. You gave your voice to the
youth of Sydney and let your mouth speak
the words they needed to hear.

You gave them your legacy.

And as the world remembers you through
your legacy, I will remember you as the
small thirteen year old boy who held
kindness in his eyes and a thirst for
adventure on his tongue. The boy who

struggled with controlling his demons and so he became one.

The camera in your hand was just an extension of you, of who you were in this world.

I will forever remember the endless conversations we had about chasing our dreams and carving our names into this earth's history.
The midnight calls when it was quiet and all you wanted to do was ride your skateboard and talk.

The plans to travel the world and explore everything we could while we still had the chance. The endless summer we all had together when we were drunk on our youth and hopeful for what the future would bring.

That summer is a feeling that will last forever.

Your art is the legacy the youth will keep, and the little boy with a skateboard and big dreams is the legacy I will keep.

Forever thinking of you,

Your Eleanor & Park girl

CHAPTERS

Chapter 1

The Leaves Are Falling And So Must I

He had that
Cosmic energy
Deep in
The creases
Of his lips,

It felt like
Kissing the universe

Darling,
Let's dive into
The Milky Way
And swim

My toes curled
When you smiled
And told me
"This moment feels like forever"

I have wasted away years
Reaching for the sky
Wanting to taste so desperately
The colours of the sunset

But darling,
I have found the sunset
Making a home of itself
In the depths of your eyes

The world sleeps softly
Beneath our grass stained feet
Your lips curled into a smile
And in that moment
I just know
I wouldn't be anywhere else

The first glimmers
Of the morning sun
Slowly stretch
Across the indigo sky

And just like a new day
It had felt like a new beginning
When I watched you
Softly sleeping beside me

Your face peaceful and content
In the realms of your dreams
And I couldn't help but smile
Thinking this would last

It was wild, knowing that this
Was our first time meeting and yet
I felt that I'd somehow
Known you my entire life

Tell me, do you feel it too?

Like a child's first breath
I am reborn again
In every moment I find you

All I'd wanted in that moment
Was to lay beside you
And kiss every freckle
That painted itself onto your flesh
Like burning stars in the night sky

We were tipsy from our youth
With tongues that tasted of wine
And eyes that were made to watch sunsets

Sometimes when I'm feeling nostalgic
Thinking of the years long past
I remember you the way
I had seen you then
Your face glowing
Underneath the warm sunlight
Sitting beside me on a park bench
Laughing with that
Boyish charm you'd had
And it makes me smile
Knowing I'll always have
That picture painted
Into my memory

I'm so grateful to know
That I am capable of
Loving someone so fully
And passionately that it
Fills my body with
Butterflies from head to toe
To know that I am small in size
But that my heart exists greater
Than any gravitational weight

It was a strong feeling
An energy I felt
Only around you
That transcended any
Description I could think of

They say that if you
Are loved by a writer
You will never die
And so I hope that me loving you
Grants you the luxury
And grace of immortality
You'll live through the pages
That echo of your voice
You'll breathe the words
I wrote of you
Like I breathed your presence
You will be forever young
With every word read
And even when I am no longer present
The world will still know of you
They will know of the intensity in your
eyes
When you stared into mine
Or how your lips always tasted
Like a distant memory
As if I'd known my whole life
How they would taste

Don't fret my darling
We'll be together again
Not in this lifetime
In another somewhere
Far away from here

This moment here
As our eyes meet
This is all that matters

Down by the river
The sun kissed your skin
So beautifully
When you turned to me
And showed me the world
In your eyes

Hold me so tight
That our bodies
Melt into one another's
As if they were meant
To create one being

I sat by the ocean and
Whispered to the waves
We were drunk on
Stories of summer
When I'd told them
All about you
They had glittered
Underneath the sunlight
Wishing me a love
Deeper than theirs
With the shore

The rain covered us in seconds
Thick and heavy on our clothes
Our drenched hair clung to our faces
And there was a slight shiver
In the way you held me
Close to your chest

You screamed to hear yourself
Over the sound of raindrops
Pelting the ground surrounding us
And then you laughed
Almost childlike in your wonder
And suddenly I found myself
Understanding the simple beauty
Of standing in the rain

What an honour it is
To know I am a chapter
In the making of
Your life's history

Tell me a story about
The moon and the sun
How there is stardust
Speckled across our very flesh
Tell me why I'm sitting here
Beside you on this beach
And how were able to
Have lived in the same millennium
And will die in the same together
Tell me you're a man of science
Yet even you are struck by silence
At the sheer dumb luck of this
Meeting of two souls drifting
Amidst billions

They clung to one another
Moulded into each other's figures
As if pieces stuck together
To create one sculpture in time

I whispered for him
To call my name
And when he did
It was as if hearing it
Through new ears
As if I'd never heard
Anything
Until that moment
When he'd sung it
As if it were a song

His eyes weren't a blue as soft as the sky
Or a green that whispered of the forest
They were black
But they weren't just black
They were the crashing waves of the
ocean
When it was dark and the world was
asleep
His eyes were the shadow amongst
The graveyard of stars
And the penetrating stare of the raven
They were so much than
Just black

She couldn't help but notice the way her heart almost skipped a beat, grasping the flowing material of her sundress just a little bit tighter into her fist. Maybe it was the way the summer heat ignited her flesh like gasoline, or the way her name sounded so light bouncing off of his tongue, almost childlike in a way.

His eyes were
Ever so calculating
As if they were trying
To uncover the cosmos
Hidden underneath my flesh

I'd never been the one to believe or trust
in a god. But darling, the closest to
religion I'd ever felt was on that one
sunny afternoon, where you kissed me by
the river and said this could be it.

We weren't designed to last
And I can accept that
As long as you promise
That when your hands
Are wrinkled with time
Your hair the shade of
Pearls in the sun
And your soft eyes
Tell of a life lived too well
You will remember us
Just as we were before
Drunk on our youth
And our infinite capacity to love

Hearing you laugh so fully
Even silenced the songbirds
Who sat atop the branches
In complete awe of you

There was something
So inexplicably French
About the way
He'd looked at me

Chapter 2

An Internal Winter

The sorrow burst through
Her lips like fire
The flames licking at her body
She shut her eyes tightly
Willing her mind to escape
The heated gaze
Eyes dancing along
Her broken frame

Like a reversed piece of art
All my bold colours
Splattered over a white canvas
Vanishing
Quicker and quicker till nothing is left
But the absence of life
Till I am a blank canvas

I am not nothing
But I feel nothing
And after every flaw in my character
This is what should fear me

And yet I envelop myself
With the aesthetics of the senses
Cover my sins with the fabric of time
The less I feel
The more the canvas becomes
A blank expression
It is not me anymore

He's talented at hiding his emotions
Practicing since he was a child
Watching and learning how not to trust
How not to let others get too close
Eyes kept directly on the
Broken marriage in front of him
Thinking that maybe this is
All love was supposed to be

It's heartbreaking, isn't it?
The way I look for you
In every crowd I see
Desperately searching
But never finding

I never understood
The laughter of Icarus
As he plummeted into
The mouth of the flames

As if there was a sense of
Poetic justice in falling
When you should be flying

Yet suddenly
I met you
And it all made
Perfect sense

And for now I'll make a home
Of the arms that hold me
Because it's cold and I'm scared
Of what tomorrow may bring

I think I loved you
Because you were
A reflection of me

Like shards of glass
Glued back together
But the scars always there
Etched permanently

And I never could resist
A broken thing
I thought I could fix

It's a tragic feeling
Knowing that
Yesterday
I was the moon and stars
But today
I'm just a stranger
With all your secrets

Something inside is hurting
And I'm frightened
What if Van Gogh was right?

What if
The sadness really
Does last
Forever?

Oh to lose myself
In a world
Of my own destruction

It's sad really
I have so much love to give
Yet it falls in the hands
Of people not meant for me
Every time

I was ten years old
When mother nature
Decided my body
Was ready to transcend
Into womanhood
I was eleven years old
When boys in my class
Took notice of the breasts
Growing on my chest
And began to change
Their behavior around me
I was twelve years old
When I first felt the discomfort
Of a grown man's
Lustful gaze on me
As if he had been lost
In the deserts for days
And my youthfulness
Was the first fresh feast
He'd laid eyes upon
In what felt like forever

'You're okay, everything will be okay."
She'd cried to her reflection in the glass.

"Everything will be okay."

It was both impressive and pitiful
The speed at which she hid
Her dried up tears
Remnants of heartache spilled
Across the floor like a bottle of wine
And painted her face with
The prettiest of illusions
A smile

How do I say goodbye
If I haven't finished
Saying hello?

He saw her
One version of her
And thought
He knew all of her

There was nothing that
You could have asked for
That I would not have given
And you relished in that power
You asked for my heart
So I ripped it out and
Begged for you to take it
Blood dripping down my fingers

Then you asked for my faith
And I dropped to the floor
Thanking the universe for you
It was when you sought for
Total power over my mind
That the fog grew clearer
And I came to the
Crushing realisation
This was not love

I'm tired of feeling trapped
As if staying here any longer
Is killing me softly but surely
I long to see the world
With my rose tinted eyes
And feel freedom the way
It demands to be felt

I have reduced myself to the seabed
I lay low with the peaceful waves
And wait for night to creep up
Before I join with the crashing
Of the sharp, deadly waves

It seems my body does not understand
That I cannot keep falling
Into the comfort of your chains

I often dream of her
A girl I'd once known
In a time far from here
She'd carried the world
On her fragile shoulders
Until the burden was too heavy
For her to hold on her own
Her eyes slowly turned dull
Smiles practiced in front of a mirror
As if she'd known something
None of us had known yet
And so she'd lived and died
Too quickly and too terribly young
Leaving behind a haunting corpse
Reminiscent of such youth and beauty

Like a prisoner yearning
To never escape
I am running
As fast as I can
Only I am running
Towards you

The realisation terrifies me
Leaves me wide awake in
The dead of night to know
That I must live in a world
Which you are not in

The thought comes and goes
Sickening me to my core
That just maybe
In decades far away
I will sit in a cushioned chair
Wrinkled with the age of time

And look back nostalgically
At my distant youth
And see a particular photograph
Of a terribly handsome boy
With a breathtaking smile

And I will struggle to remember
What that boy's name was
I am so fucking frightened
That one day I might possibly
Forget your name, Ian

Darling, I see you
So afraid to let yourself feel
Your eyes are glistening
And your lips are trembling
There's an ache throbbing
In your palms and chest
And it's so deafening to your ears
Everything feels so smothered

I see you because I was you
And I know it is exhausting
To live like this constantly
I wish I could hold you in my arms
But I'm afraid I cannot
I am merely the words on this page
So I'll say this for now
I hope your pain will ease one day

For just one night
Let us pretend that it's
Love that we are feeling
And you and I
Are what each other needs

They're both exhausted
I see it in their eyes
And the deep shadows
Those mark their faces
All too telling of lives
Spent living for the sake of others
Sacrificed what felt like everything
So that their children
And their children after them
Could possess the freedom
To think and act and speak
In ways they were forbidden
Back in their war torn homes

You look at me
And only see
What you choose to

It's a dangerous thing
Falling for the idea
Of someone
It's easy to love an illusion
And painful to understand
That some people
Can never be what
We want them to be

When you're young
No one truly prepares you
For the world you enter
And how quickly you
Feel it pass by

The mind is a dangerous thing
It can sew together entire worlds
And stack fantasies up like towers
It can lull you into a peaceful slumber
And shatter everything in seconds
Do not underestimate its power

I remember it all too well
The feeling of complete dread
That crept its way underneath my skin
As I watched you leave
You were gone and yet

The sun fell and rose once more
The waves shifted back and forth
Endlessly as they always had
The earth was still spinning
The world continued to exist
After you had left

But I was still rooted deep in soil of the
past
And it terrified me for a moment
To think that maybe
Just maybe
I was left behind

What felt like years were really months
As I felt the earth slowly untether me
From the memories that bled onto my
flesh

And console me in her tender arms
Whispering softly in my dirt streaked hair
"You will never be left behind'"

She promised me
As I wept in her arms

He was a broken boy
Trying to fit into a mold
Created for him by others
Wanting so desperately
To become a man his mother
Could someday be proud of

I remember the day I called you
 Your breaths were staggered
And you choked back a sob
You asked me about my day
I told you it was fine, but that
This call would be the highlight
I told you that I loved you

Later that week
We sat beside one another
On the small park bench
And you confessed in a whisper
That the pressure was unbearable

You were on that rooftop
With the world weighing down on you
Your fingers were trembling
When your phone had rung
And you saw it was my name

You told me that I'd saved you
As you cried in my arms
That I'd kept you from oblivion
But don't you see?
It was your decision to answer
You chose to live instead
You saved yourself all this time

I see her quite often
The girl in my dreams
She looks like me sometimes
And thinks like me too
But something is not the same

She has not had the same life
The same opportunities as I've had
I find myself at a loss of what to say
She just smiles and says it's okay
To live this life full for her too

So she can watch me and feel proud
Knowing that I carried her with me
Every step I took outside my home
And I'm grateful for this life I have
And to share this experience with her

But it confuses me as to why
I get to be in complete control of my life
And she is oppressed in her home
Where is the justice in that?

It's strange to think
Anyone could love you
So differently
To see parts of you
That I'll never see

It was beautiful while it lasted
But you're hurting me
And I can't stay and watch
As you turn to me
Thinking just one more chance
 I won't hurt anymore
Maybe you could have loved me
The way I needed you to

You weren't ready for me
For someone who could see
Past all your disguises
You weren't ready to be
Vulnerable with me
Because you were brought up
To believe that real men
Needed to be strong
And if you broke down
In front of me
What would that make you?
Human, I would have said
If you'd asked me before you left

My father spent the first
Forty years of his life
Living in a shell of himself
Raised to think but never to feel
Until he came home to this new land
And every emotion he had hid
From himself his whole life
Had burst through his lips
As though yearning to fly free
Of the chains that fought him to keep still

I remember the way
Your eyes shone
As you would talk
About your future
And the life you had
Dreamed for yourself
Outside of this place
That's why it aches me
To see you now, years later
A shell of the boy I had known
Molding yourself into someone else
To fit someone else's dreams

She was thirteen and I was fourteen
When she'd told me
She wanted to die
We wept in each other's arms afterwards
Mourning an innocence taken away from
us
So quickly and as we were so young
Yet it had felt as if we had lived a lifetime
In that moment of honesty

He told me how he loved
His mother for giving him life
And the shame he felt
When he didn't want this
Gift any longer
As if he'd let her down
He whispered these words
Almost afraid that if he
Spoke too loudly
The tears glistening in his eyes
Would become too real

I saw it in your eyes
Even as you smiled
And told me you were fine
You were struggling to
Keep it all together
So afraid to let yourself
Slip in front of others
While you mourned in secret
For the life you'd felt
In your womb one day
And how it was gone the next
As if it were never there to them
But you knew what they didn't
And it tore at your spirit

She never knew how to articulate her grief into words, so she threw herself into her art, and let the brushes act as her voice.

I begged her to leave him
To choose herself over the relationship
But he'd stripped her of
Her self love and confidence
Until she was naked and vulnerable
Thinking she couldn't live her life
Without him in it any longer
So when he had left
And she was confronted by the girl
She'd seen in the mirror
The realisation that she'd forgotten
How to love herself without him
In the picture was frightening

I'm so sorry that you do not see
Yourself the way I see you
If only I could lend you my eyes
So you'd see just how loved you are

She was raised in a society where
reputation was all you'd had, so it comes
as no surprise when she warns me to be
cautious of the clothes I wear, for it might
give the people an idea of me she dreaded.

Tell me about
Your mother
And how you
Look at her
With eyes that
Are afraid
Tell me how
You love her so
And it keeps you
Awake in the night
Knowing that one day
She won't be there
To call you back home

We're told to grieve those we lose
When their time to return to the
Earth is called, but I never knew
I'd lose someone like this
Tell me please
How do I mourn someone who isn't dead?

There is much I want to say
Not for you to hear
But for myself to listen

They may have forgiven me
But had I forgiven myself?

It is getting harder to breathe
As if the noise around me
Is filling up the space in my lungs
Suffocating me slowly
I feel so helpless
Trapped in this sensation
Of drowning without water
Stuck in an endless loop
One wave after another

You're terrified of loneliness
I could see it in your eyes
When he said his quick goodbyes
And you were left with no one
But the broken girl in the mirror
Hidden beneath the beautiful lies
Tell me why it hurt so much
For you to be alone with yourself
Tell me why you ran away
Into the arms of someone else
Not caring who it really was
Just knowing it was someone
Other than the arms of yourself
Hiding within his love
So you wouldn't hear your cries

The very thought frightens me
That one day I will know a life
Without the affection of my mother
Or the kind eyes of my father
I understand that life goes on and so do we
But teach me how to accept this fate
Because I'm terrified of knowing
What it will feel like to lose you

It's strange
To live a future
You do not belong to

I had so desperately wanted us
To be woven from the same fabric
To be two halves of a portrait
But all we'd shared was
A sense of brokenness and
The craving to be filled
By one another's love

Chapter 3

It's Time For The Flowers To Bloom

I crave deep intimacy
Not in a sexual form
But rather the
Ghost of a touch
Between two fingers
Or your head
Resting upon my
Racing heart
And most importantly
I crave the
Whispered conversations
In the dead of night

She wore
Her strength
Like sheepskin
On a wolf

"Why do you shy away whenever our eyes meet for too long?"

"Because I haven't met anyone worth that type of naked intimacy just yet."

Do not be so generous
That you give so much
Of yourself to others
That you are left
With nothing to give
Yourself

I create waves
Ripples in the water
Underneath my fingertips

Poseidon's touch
Trickling down my spine
The hunger is infinite

Lips parted breathlessly
She stared with burning eyes
As the smoke rose
From her bare flesh
Like the swirls of Van Gogh

Watching with curious eyes
Droplets of water
Painted her soft flesh
Like the night stars
Of an infinite pool

Let me trace those freckles on your back
That you hate so shamefully
When they are flecks of stardust
Mapped out on your flesh
Like a mirage of the night sky

You told me you hoped
You'd find the right person
If only you'd known
That I was everything
You were looking for
And yet you were too blind
To let yourself see

You've spent your entire life
Caring for others
When will you care for yourself?

I am

Sensitive
Chaotic
Irrational
Childlike

And it is time
I start loving
Those parts of me

I was so trapped
In the idea of
Searching for
My missing half
Thinking I'd
Find it in you
When really it had
Been inside me
Calling out
For all this time

My soul is not meant
To stay in one place
It longs to escape
The confines of this room
And taste the world

We will never have finished
Building ourselves as people
So I question why you are so willing
To accept their cold judgement
As if it were a truth
When they themselves are uncertain
Of the life they are living
And the person they are seeing
When they search for someone
In the mirror at night

There is an ability I possess
To inflict wounds upon others
Just as I have been hurt
And I am human for it
Learning from my mistakes
Growing from the faults
Acknowledging the pain
I have caused
Understanding that
Perfection is never a reality

There is no greater satisfaction
Than to be so deeply immersed
In a book and lose myself
In this whole other world
That I often find myself
Not wanting to ever leave

Not everyone loves
That way that you do
And that's okay

There will come a time
When our bodies will dissolve
Back into the roots of this earth
And the world will continue to spin
As if we had never existed
So be sure to live
Your life through yourself
And not through the expectations
Of others

Learn to love yourself
Before you love another
For if you are not ready
You will break two people
Instead of just the one

This figure
With all its curves
And soft flesh
That anchors me
It is my home
I have cried
Tears of gratitude
To belong to it
It is my temple

Who are you to try to claim it as yours?

If there's a world of worlds
In this head of mine
Who's to say?
That this world we call home
Is not a mere figment
Of someone's imagination

Dear self,

I am enraptured in this journey I tread, knowing it is leading me towards you. We will one day know each other, never completely, but close enough that we understand one another, and that is beautiful.

The past year has taken my life in unexpected directions, and for that I am eternally grateful.

It was exhilarating, leaving that place behind. I was surrounded too often by those who closed their hearts and minds to the world; too afraid of what they didn't understand.

Leaving you in the past was the most freeing sensation I'd ever felt.

I used to believe in timing
That we could find the right person
At the wrong place in the wrong moment
And that one day it would be right
Everything would fall into place
I used to think this about you
Until I found myself slowly but surely
Falling out of love with you
And falling in love with the life I lived
It left me to realise that maybe
You weren't mine and I
Wasn't yours any longer
And that was okay
Not every love
We receive in life
Is right for us

I want you to inspire me
To make me feel things
I haven't felt before
Is that too much to ask of you?

There's a song in your eyes
That yearns to be sung

It was fascinating, the speed at which I found myself falling out of love with him as the days from our last goodbye grew longer. Then, and only then, was I forced to conclude that I had not loved *him*, but rather the idea of him.

As the months flew by
With nothing but my mind
Keeping me company
I was forced to recognise
My anxiety for what it was
A reaction of all the pain
I'd felt over the years
And how that gradually shaped me
Into the person I am today
I am not my anxiety
I have never let it define me
And I never plan to

Too many times that year
I wanted to make the hurting stop
To escape this darkness that had
Enveloped me completely
Body and soul
I was terrified of myself
Of my thoughts and emotions
Desperately wanting everything to stop
I am grateful that I did not listen
Proud of the girl I was
And how she had saved me from herself

Maybe we were just young fools
But I kept you in this heart of mine
And I'll cherish the memories
If you promise too

In order to forgive myself
I had to forgive you also

Why are you so content?
Repeating the actions
That no longer serve
Your needs as an individual
But rather put hold
Of the growth that is ahead

No longer pursue those who choose not to pursue you.

Wear your self respect and
Love with pride
For they may weaponise it
As steel knives dipped in
Arrogance and narcissism
If you are not certain of it's value

Do not give them the chance
To strip you of your dignity
And sense of self worth for they
Are yours and no one else's

Too many times
Have I given too much
Of myself to others
I must learn to be selfish
With how I spend my energy

Take ownership of how
You treat yourself and
Learn what must
Be unlearned

You told me
You loved me
But it just wasn't
Enough anymore
There is so much
More than just love

Own up to your pain
To your mistakes
There is courage in
Choosing when to
Take responsibility
For the actions
You have caused

What a shame it would be
To love as you do
So half heartedly

I am exhausted by their words
Telling me to 'hurry up before it's too late'
Whether I am doe eyed and fresh faced
Or my hair is the colour of pearls in the
sun
It will never be too late to start living
The life I've only ever dared to dream of
To settle for anything less than what I
deserve
Is a life half lived and half tried

When the dust settles
And they've decided that this
Is no longer what they want
That you are no longer for them
Do not lower yourself to your knees
Pleading for them to stay still
You do not need to beg for
The love you are deserving of

When I warn you to fall in love
With yourself before
You fall in love with them
It is so that if they leave one day
You will know that your world is
Still spinning and you are still alive
With or without them in it

I think I held on to you for so long
Because a part of me felt as if I were
Losing myself once I'd lost you
As if the two would go hand in hand
And it's taken me a long journey
To finally comprehend
I am not any less of myself
Without you in my life

A part of me is still weeping
Mourning the loss of a friendship
One that had grown when I
Needed it the most
I know that leaving you
In my past is the
Only way for me
To continue in my
Pursuit for peace
And I'm tired of trying
To heal someone who
Doesn't want to be healed

There are over seven billion
People in this world
And I know that none of them
Are ever going to be you
But I think that's the
Beautiful thing about change
No experience will ever
Be the same as the last

I have been slowly but surely
Removing people from my life
That do not serve to make it greater
I'm tired of being surrounded by
Those who do not support my growth
As an individual but rather
Strain my energy on the
Insignificant things and there
Is no more room for them

I think it's beautiful
The way we create meaning
In the earth
Spinning 365 times
How we strive
To better ourselves
At every mark
Of every beginning

I'm so desperate for
Deep human connection
No more space in my life
For dispassionate people

I believe that
When we see art
And cry
It is not because
It exists so beautifully
But because it
Dares to exist
So beautifully
In a world
So polluted with ugly

It is not about growing
For their sake
You must grow
For yourself
And the right person
Will gravitate towards you

The more I grow
The more aware
I slowly become
Of the roots
That birthed me

One day
You'll dream of me
And wake up startled
Wondering why
You ever let me slip
From your loose grasp

There's a sense of irony
In being a writer
And finding myself
At a loss for words

I'm at a conflicting stage
In my life currently
Feeling as if I am
Wasting precious time
And yet
There is a whole life
Ahead of me
I am yet to live

There are glimpses of the past
Seconds that feel almost immortal
That you can't help but think of
Wishing to feel those moments
Just once more as they were

You've spent your years
Working endlessly to keep
A roof above our heads
Never stopping for a second
To look at your reflection
And love yourself
The way you have loved us

And there not enough words
In the English language
That can encompass my
Gratitude for your sacrifices
Jut the mere hope
That some day soon
I'll be able to provide you
The life you so desperately deserve

I dream that someday
Hopefully soon
You'll learn to see
Yourself the way
That I see you

Instead of dropping coins into the fountain, she threw in a dozen red roses; all plucked from their stems. They spread across the crystal clear water, bathing underneath the sunlight. She then poured in a fistful of sugar. "To turn it to rose syrup." She'd hummed, smiling back at me.

My mother and father
Risked their lives to escape
Their war torn worlds
Instead choosing to raise
Their children in a world
Where options were more
Than the nudging knives
Behind their backs
Where free will and individuality
Was not spit on like
A curse of bad luck

Chapter 4

Summer Is A Feeling That Will Last Forever

I do not need you
To fill me up
I am not empty
Without you

Do not mistake
My emotions
For weakness
It is strength
To feel everything
So completely
And not crumble
From its weight

If you can not
Handle me
At my lowest
That is fine
I handle myself
At my lowest
Every time
And I
Am stronger
Than you
For it

I do not regret
The bruises and scars
That have marked my
Heart over the years

I am learning that
Failure is what
Keeps us going

Her hair flew back
As she felt the breeze
Dance across her face
The highway a blur
Of cars and flashing lights
This felt like freedom

I was born to be a writer
The feelings runs
Down to my core

I am meant to live
So much more
Than one life

I am meant to be
So much more
Than one person

You deserve the
Love you look for
In dreams

I am tired of pretending
That I am fine with casual
There is no casual in me
I am passionate and
Deeply expressive of my emotions
If that is not what you
Are searching for
That is fine
Look somewhere else
I am not for you

Do not roll your eyes
And mistake me for anything
Less than what I am
When you come to notice
I am a hopeless romantic
All the great poets are, darling

To lose oneself in aestheticism
There is nothing on this earth
Worth pursuing more
Than to appreciate art
For art's sake

There is something magical
When a sculptor can
Carve through stone
And turn it to soft flesh
As if he were a god
Birthing humans from rocks

I am not responsible
For their opinions
Of my character
The only opinion of me
Which holds any significance
Is my own

I am in awe of the life that surrounds you,
the same way the bees gravitate towards
the sunflowers.

There is something so beautiful to me, in the way people sit and wait to watch the sun as it sets. And how they wake up the next morning, just as eager to watch it rise once more. This sun is the god they worship, boundless from any religion.

The sunlight feels different on the skin,
when you're by the ocean tide.

Surround yourself with freely thinking individuals, and watch the way your world transforms.

Do you hear that?
The way the ocean
Sings so softly
As it pulls to the shore

I remember her
The girl I was before
Sometimes I can feel her
Calling out to me
In my reflection
Asking me to forgive her
For not loving herself enough
'Silly girl' I whisper to her
Do not apologise
I have enough love
For the both of us

Leaving that place behind
And entering the world that awaited me
Allowed me to truly recognise
Just how euphoric it can feel
No longer finding myself bound
To people who thrived on toxicity
It was in every sense of the word
Freeing

It is absolutely fascinating
The raw power of music
It brings us back to moments
Long forgotten in the past
And sparks us to feel
What we have not in years
This is when you truly feel time

She reminded me of sunflowers in the springtime. Something was so indescribably yellow about her soul, and I couldn't help but feel haunted by it.

I want to bathe in milk
And feed myself grapes
To wrap myself in robes
And sip on glasses of wine
Until the warmth slowly
Seeps into my flesh

I want to feel like a goddess

She was so remarkably good
Even the tears that slipped
Across her plump cheeks
Were of sweet rosewater

What a tragedy it would be
To live a life so half heartedly
I wish to spend the rest of my days
So fully and passionately
That when the evening sun sets
And my time in this body is over
I will laugh and look back fondly
Then take death's tender hand
As if it were a dear friend's

I have but one heart
It will not be wasted
In the hands of those
Blind to its significance

The world is wide
And it's calling for me
To lose myself
In the midst of it all

I sat there on the sand
My eyes closed as I
Soaked up the warmth
Of the sunlight dancing
Across my bare face
Listening to the waves
Crash and fall as they do
And found myself at a loss
Of words in the moment
For what felt like hours
Were only fleeting seconds

I want to lay atop an open field of grass
In the middle of nowhere with no one
And see the stars the way they long to be
seen

It's an exhilarating sensation
To know that outside of here
Is a world beyond both our
comprehension

I was 19 when I saw
The sky for the first time
A world away from
The lights of any city
Sitting on a damp patch of grass
Seemingly nowhere in no time
It brought me to tears
The way the stars softly sung to me
As if they knew we were meant to
Meet one another this way

I will not make myself small
To let you feel big

You are a visitor
To this body I call home
Do not overstay your welcome

The birds chirped away
As the radio continued to sing
And the wind decided to dance
Finding delight in the sound
We liked to call 'summer'

'I'm so sorry it took me
So long to learn to love you.'
The words came out softly
Afraid to become more than a whisper
As I watched my body weep in glee

It took me years
To recognise my worth
Took all the strength and
Love I had left in me
To worship myself like
The goddess I was becoming
So as you try to tear through me
I must warn you, my darling
You cannot break what has been
Built from the ashes of its past
There is too much power in the woman
Who learns to love herself as she is

The rains was heavy
As it kissed my fingertips
My arms stretched out to feel
In the fresh awakening of spring
The song of the streaming river
Blending into the splattering rain
And I thought to myself
What greater gift can we receive?
Than the softness of Mother Earth
As she tells us her becoming story
By way of the life that surrounds us?

If you no longer want this
Us
I will not beg you to stay
If you cannot love me more
I love myself enough
To know I will be okay
Without you

Who are we to claim the earth as ours?
As we build roads and towers
Upon gardens older than you
And I and our ancestors
Our time here is fleeting
A blink in the great vastness of time
The story of Mother Earth does not
Finish with us for
We are merely her guests
Treat her with the respect she is owed

I forgive you for not loving me
To the capacity that I am worthy of
I now understand that not everyone
Can love the way that I do
And when it is right one day
I will be met with the fierceness of a love
That will make anything else I had
Felt before feel insignificant in
comparison

I was never intimidating
You just could not comprehend
How powerful of a woman I truly am
And it terrified you to realise
That I never needed you

I am so proud of
The you that you are becoming
As if you are finally returning
Home to yourself
After all these years of
Tirelessly seeking shelter
In the arms of others

Surround yourself with those
Who think differently and freely
For it would be a crime against nature
To limit yourself to the circle
Of those who choose
Not to think but
Forget how to live

Our time on this earth is fleeting
Finishing with every breathe we take
Why must we live it in any other way
Than the one we so desperately want to?

I pity those who
In becoming part of society
Lose themselves along the way
It does not do to
Belong to others and
Not yourself

You stared and
Questioned me
Relentlessly
Bewildered in the
Possibility that I
Could be an Iraqi woman
And not belong
To any religion
As if my Arab identity
Was missing something
Without
As if believing in a god
Was expected of me
Tell me then
Why do I need a god
When there is already
A goddess within me?

I want to see and appreciate art
To hear music and dance and sing
To taste the world through
Food and travelling
I just want to live my life
So full of experiences
That when it's time for me
To return to the earth
I am content with the
Memories buried with me

Living is too brief and breathtaking of an experience to waste it on a life you were never meant for.

There is an entire generation
Of Arab women who have
Yet to be born
I am shaking with anticipation
To see the force of change
They will birth with them

Do you hear it?
The music
It's playing
So softly
And yet
Do you feel it?
The way the rhythm
Speaks to your heart
As if it's calling you
Home

It is okay to feel uncertain
Of what you want in this life
There is no one way of living
No one person you must be
That is what makes life
So beautiful
The ability to feel
And act and change
As much as we choose to

It's truly fascinating
The way we often forget
How much life truly surrounds us
How each and every single
One of us holds an entire
World in our minds
Living an entire life
Separate from each other's

There is a stranger walking past me
A stranger who has lovers
And enemies
And friendship
And trauma
Just a completely different person
With an entirely unique way of thinking

I am excited and anxious
For the day that I become her
The old woman sitting beneath
The shaded tree on a park bench
Sharing my stories and experiences
With anyone who walks by
And chooses to listen

It brought me to tears
Seeing another sharing
Her experiences in her art
Exposing herself to vulnerability
Living in a world that was
Frowned upon and embracing
Her identity as an Arab and a woman
But most important of all
Embracing herself
Faults and all

The way the wind
Hums of a song
Long forgotten
How the waves
Crash in remembrance
Of a time only to be traced
By the vast sea
There is something
So marvelous in the
Great vastness of
Time and space
And so completely
Humbling in the realisation
Of the insignificance
Of humankind

He saw my collection of books
And chuckled to himself
Believing I was silly
For wasting away in literature
And forgetting to enjoy
The world that was around me
I laughed terribly and
Out of pity
For it must be
Quite a sad existence
To live in one ordinary world
And be blind to the possibilities
Of travelling to entirely different
Dimensions of life
When one only dares
To turn to the next page

I am slowly but surely
Becoming the woman
I am supposed to be
It is a thrilling sensation
To reach a point where
I finally understand
I am the love of my life

What a dreadful experience
It would be to deprive oneself
From the pleasures of reading
And remain in a world
Where the air is still and
Magic is a word of child's play

It's the 2nd of October
The year is 2020
It's 5 o'clock in the evening
And the birds are humming
The sunlight is dancing
Among the tree leaves
There are crowds of people
Walking past as they go
All on their way to
Somewhere
A young girl is singing
Beautifully down the street
And I'm sitting on the same
Park bench as we used to
Alone this time
With a book in my hand
And the thought comes
To me like smoke
How very different
Life can be when
You just let it

I used to care so desperately
For the approval of others
Thinking I would be satisfied
If they were too
Thinking I would find
Myself through them
But I'm here now
Loving myself and
Learning to love my faults
The only opinion I need
Is my own

You told me that my character
Was 'too much' for you
I was too loud and too terribly optimistic
Too obsessed with things
But darling
Maybe it was just you?
I remember viewing your words
As sharp steel bullets
Digging into the dips of my back
Now they're scented flowers
Sitting in a glass vase atop the dining table
It is a wondrous thing
To be so loud and full of music
So optimistic and spread joy
And so deeply passionate for
The things in life that make me happy

It says more about their character
Than it does for yours
When they say such
Hateful slurs to you
So lift your chin up darling
And remind yourself that
It is better to have lived
So completely and authentically yourself
Than to have hidden away
Underneath the insignificant
Words of others

I'm here and I see you
And I promise that there is
A world of worlds out there
Waiting for you to grab it
By your shaking hands

How exhilarating it must feel
To be a bird bound to no land
Or place in time
To live among the breeze
And feel the warmth of the sun
So constantly as if it were a friend

There was the sound of French music
Playing softly in our ears as we
Strolled down the cobblestone road
Giggling to ourselves as we shared
A bottle of sauvignon
Pretending we were walking in Paris
Drunkenly admiring the way
The lights seemed to glow
Underneath the darkened sky
And I thought to myself
This right here
This is what life is made of
Little moments where we
Truly lose our selves to joy

There is an indescribable feeling
When one unfolds the skeleton of a book
And finds themselves entirely lost
In worlds quite unlike their own

I'm eternally grateful for her
The broken girl I used to see
In my reflections
Her eyes were dull
And she was no longer content
To stay in this place
A cage of her own making
But something convinced her
To break out and keep living
Something told her what
She'd be missing if she quit
And I'm sitting here
Absolutely in love with
The memories I have made
And have yet to create
All I'm thinking about is her
She stayed so that I could live
For the both of us
I intend to make her proud

"What if your relatives overseas see that picture?"

"That shirt is showing too much, don't you think?"

"Don't drink too much, it's not a nice image to have."

"You shouldn't go on too many dates with different men, you'll look too loose."

But don't you see?
I am so much more than
Their uncomfortable staring
So much more than
The judgement of relatives
I've never met before
So much more than
Just a body that is sexualized
So much more than
An Arab woman that is not fit
To your expectations
Of what an Arab woman is supposed to be

I am the poetry I write in my room
The music I dance and sing along to

When I'm cooking in the kitchen and
No one is watching
The laughter I share with friends
On a night out
The conversations I have
About life and death
The romances I have experienced
And the endless memories
I have made so far
I am so much more than
What you see or think

I am not interested in pursuing anything
That does not ignite a passion in me so
strong
That I am moved to tears

The tequila was strong on my tongue
Body pulsing to the beat of the music
There was a scent of summer sweat in the
air
And I closed my eyes as I kept dancing
Feeling myself let go of control
Nothing could come between
The music and I in that moment
A greater romance than the history pages

Your body is more than
What society believes it to be
It is an entire symphony orchestra
Comprised of numerous instruments
And sounds that work so
Desperately in unity with one another
Achieving the most beautiful
Experience imaginable
So be sure to appreciate
Each and every part that makes you
Listen to their soft melody
For it is the concoction of hard work
And complete devotion to you

Hopelessly devoted to creating
The life I've always wanted

There is something so
Rebellious and thrilling
About being an Arab woman
In the western world
To be constantly judged
And whispered about
By the prying eyes of
Both men and women alike
And laugh in the face of
Their traditional expectations
As I sip my mojito in
All its sinful glory and
Continue to dance in my
Terribly short skirt

I am entirely designed
From the galaxy
Stitched together with
Scraps of planets that
Were never made
Of stardust left over
From explosions
So who are you?
To think that I owe you
Any part of me
When I am the daughter
Birthed from the universe

I should not have to choose
Between being an Arab woman
And a western woman
There is no absolute reason I see
That dictates I cannot go out
Dancing in the city till the crack of dawn
Drunk on my youth and freedom
Then return home and
Drink chai with my knafeh
There is too much living
I must leave my mark on
To be left spending my years
In the cage of your judgements

An ode to 'Eib' by Sarah Bahbah

She was as soft
As the petals that fell from
The cherry blossom trees
And as fierce as
The storm that pillages
And leaves wreckage in its path
She is Persephone
Brought to the 21st century

There is so much life
We have yet to live
Are you ready for it?

There is an infinite capacity of growth
I have yet to face and I'm not
Ashamed to admit there is much
In me that is still learning
How to exist in this world

Who are you in this existence?
When it is time to leave and
You are left with nothing
But your memories?

Author's Note

I hope you have reached this point of the
book, knowing that you and I are now
bonded. Sharing myself with you so
intimately, we are almost lovers.

Remember me in that way, I ask you.
Remember me as the lover you swore
stole your heart and wrecked it in the
space of a few pages.

I want to know I exist somewhere in your
mind forever, no matter how tight or
spacious the room is for me to rest.
Whether it is haunting you or comforting
you, I am there now.

Hanging up portraits on the walls of your
inner mind and arranging fresh flowers
around the space. Making a home inside
of your thoughts.

Until the next,

Bella.

Made in the USA
Columbia, SC
21 March 2021

34182523R00145